UnMuted

Find Your Voice Against Bullying

SAMRIDHI SHARMA

Made with ❤ on the Notion Press Platform
www.notionpress.com

To every teen who has ever felt unseen,
unheard, or alone.

You are strong, you are worthy,
and your scars shine brightly.

This book is for you.

"You will always be criticized and teased and bullied for things that make you different, but usually those things will be what set you apart. The things that set you apart from the pack, the things that you once thought were your weaknesses will someday become your strengths."

– Taylor Swift

Contents

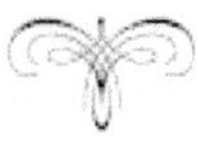

CONTENTS

Prologue

Ever walked through the school corridors with that knot in your stomach? Maybe you see a group huddled together, whispering and giggling. Or perhaps you hear a cruel nickname echo down the hallway, leaving you feeling exposed.

Bullying doesn't have to be a movie scene with shoved lockers and ripped clothes. In India, it can sneak in like a rumour on a hidden social media chat, or a sly comment about your looks. It can be the constant feeling of being left out or targeted because you're 'different.'

This booklet is your guide to navigating the school corridor shuffle. We'll decode the different types of bullying, show you how to stand up for yourself and others, and most importantly, remind you that you're NOT alone.

About Guzaarish Foundation:

Guzaarish Foundation, a compassionate organisation working across India and parts of Nepal, is dedicated to creating a safer and more positive world. We believe that everyone deserves to feel empowered and free from bullying. It is founded by Samridhi Sharma, the author of the book.

@GUZAARISHFOUNDATION

If you've been bullied and want to share your story, or if you're facing challenges right now and need someone to talk to, don't hesitate to reach out to Guzaarish Foundation. We offer a safe space for you to connect and find support. Feel free to DM us on Instagram.

1

Ugh! You're Not Alone: Dealing with Bullies

It starts subtly, disguised as friendly teasing. Maybe your 'friends' make fun of your braces, constantly pointing at them or calling you nicknames related to them. Perhaps they poke fun at features they perceive as different, resorting to insensitive nicknames or comments about your height or complexion.

They know exactly what buttons to push. At first, you brush it off, thinking it's just playful banter. It takes a lot of strength to act unfazed when someone is making you feel bad. But inside, you know it hurts. But then, things escalate.

They start making demands. "Copy my homework" or "Tell that teacher we're not prepared for the test," they might say. If you don't comply, you're suddenly the 'coward' or the 'teacher's pet.' The teasing gets harsher, with jabs about your grades, your hobbies, or even who you have a crush on. You try to fight back with witty remarks, but it just fuels the fire.

You're confused. These are your 'friends,' right? Shouldn't friendship feel good? But the constant jabs, manipulation, and feeling unsafe leave you drained and isolated. It's hard to see the bigger picture when you're caught in the cycle.

This isn't friendship; this is **'BULLYING,'** and it sucks. The truth is, most of these 'friends' probably don't even see you as an equal. They feed off your discomfort for their own amusement.

Now you might be wondering, isn't bullying always physical, like shoving someone in the hallway? Or maybe you're thinking, 'Isn't this just what friends do sometimes?'

Bullying is actually the repeated use of words or actions to hurt someone, both physically and emotionally. It can happen anywhere, at school, online, or even at home. The key thing is that it's **intentional** and **repeated.** It's not a one-time fight or a playful joke that goes too far.

Bullies come in all shapes and sizes, and they can use different tactics to make you feel bad.

Types of Bullying:

- **Verbal:** Name-calling, insults, put-downs, threats.
- **Physical:** Shoving, hitting, tripping, stealing belongings.
- **Social:** Excluding you from activities, spreading rumours, making fun of you in front of others.
- **Cyberbullying:** Using technology to bully someone online, like sending nasty messages or posting embarrassing photos.

No matter what kind of bullying you're facing, it's important to know that **you're not alone**. In the next chapter, we'll explore ways to deal with bullies and build healthy friendships.

Chapter Reflections

Chapter Reflections

2

You Got This! Standing Up to Bullies

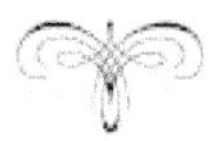

Remember that feeling? The knot in your stomach, the tightness in your throat, the sinking feeling when you realised you were being targeted. We talked in Chapter 1 about how bullying can sneak up in disguise, making it hard to recognise at first. Maybe it started with 'friendly' teasing from classmates that turned mean-spirited. Perhaps you were pressured to do things you weren't comfortable with or excluded from activities you enjoyed.

Whatever form it took, bullying can make you feel isolated, confused, and even scared. The good news is, you **don't** have to deal with bullying by yourself. This chapter is all about empowering YOU to stand up to bullies and take back control. We'll explore different strategies you can use, from simply ignoring a bully's taunts to using humour to deflect their attacks. We'll also talk about the importance of having a strong support system and why speaking up to a trusted adult is the bravest thing you can do.

By the end of this chapter, you'll be equipped with the tools and confidence to deal with bullies in a healthy way. Remember, **YOU are NOT alone,** and there are people who care about you and want to help.

Understanding Bullies (Super Quick!)

Bullies might be going through something tough themselves. They might feel insecure or powerless, and picking on others can make them feel better (even if it's just for a short while.) Knowing this doesn't mean their behaviour is okay. It just means they might need help too. But the most important thing is **YOU.**

The truth is, you deserve to be treated with respect, no matter what someone else is going through. So, let's move on to the most important part: **Strategies for Standing Up to Bullies** and taking back control of the situation!

Here's your toolbox filled with different techniques you can use depending on the situation:

- **The Ignore Option:** This can be a good strategy for occasional teasing or comments that don't bother you much. Act like you didn't hear them and walk away with your head held high. But remember, if the bullying keeps happening or gets worse, ignoring it won't make it stop. Time to choose another tool!

- **The Confident Reply:** Sometimes, the best way to deal with a bully is to stand your ground and use your voice. Here are some tips:

- **Speak Up:** Use a firm voice and clear language. Say things like "Stop it. That's not funny" or "Leave me alone."

- **Body Language Matters:** Stand tall, make eye contact (if you feel safe), and don't fidget. Project confidence even if you're feeling nervous inside.

- **Practice Makes Perfect:** Role-playing with a friend or family member can help you practice using confident replies in different situations.

- **Humour with a Punch:** This can be a tricky one, but sometimes using humour can take the power away from a bully's words. Here's the key: use jokes that are kind and don't make fun of the bully themselves. A witty comeback can leave the bully speechless and show them their taunts aren't getting to you. (e.g., "Is that the best you can come up with?")

Remember: Don't use mean jokes or insults back. That can make things worse.

- **The "I Won't Tell" Strategy:** Bullies often try to keep their victims quiet by saying things like "If you tell anyone, I'll..." Don't be afraid to tell someone you trust, like a teacher, counsellor, or parent. You're not a 'tattletale' for speaking up. It's important to get help so the bullying can stop.

Remember: These are just some tools you can use. The best strategy might depend on the situation and how you feel comfortable reacting. If you ever feel unsafe, walk away and find a trusted adult.

We'll explore the importance of having a strong support system in the next section, but for now, you've got this! Keep your head held high and don't let bullies bring you down.

Imagine having a whole team of people cheering you on, ready to back you up no matter what. A group of friends, family, and mentors who believe in you and have your back – that's what a support system is all about! Think of them as your own personal superhero squad, ready to swoop in and help whenever you need it.

This chapter is all about building this amazing support system. We'll explore why it's important, who can be part of it, and how you can create strong connections with these awesome people. By the end, you'll know exactly how to build your own squad – a powerful team that will help you navigate anything life throws your way, including those pesky bullies!

Chapter Reflections

Chapter Reflections

3

You've Got My Back: The Power of a Support System

Remember that fist-pumping feeling you had after conquering Chapter 2? You learned awesome strategies to stand up to bullies, and that's a superpower all on its own! But guess what can make those skills even more epic? Having a rock-solid support system behind you.

Think of your support system like your own personal Justice League (or Avengers, if you prefer!) These are the friends, family members, and teachers who are always in your corner, no matter what life throws your way. They're the ones who high-five your victories, cheer you on through challenges, and are there to catch you if you stumble.

This chapter is all about building that amazing support system. We'll explore why it's important, who can be part of your squad, and how to build strong connections with them. By the end, you'll be ready to assemble your own team of awesome people who will have your back, not just when dealing with bullies, but throughout all of life's adventures!

What is a Support System?

Imagine you're playing your favourite sport. You might be a total rock star on the field, but even the most skilled athletes need a team behind them. Referees make sure the game is fair, coaches offer guidance and motivation, and teammates have your back when things get tough.

Your support system is kind of like your off-the-field team in the game of life. These are the people **who care about you, believe in you, and are always there to cheer you on.** They're the ones you can confide in about anything, even the tough stuff, because you know they'll listen without judgement.

A support system can be big or small, but it's always made up of people who make you feel good about yourself. They're the ones who **celebrate your successes**, no matter how big or small, and **help you pick yourself up** when you're feeling down.

Why is a Support System Important?

Having a strong support system is like having a secret weapon in your life's backpack. It can help you in so many ways, especially when dealing with bullies. Here's why having a squad of awesome people on your side is super important:

- **Boosts Your Confidence:** Knowing you have a team cheering you on makes you feel stronger and more capable of facing challenges, big or small. It's like having a built-in pep talk whenever you need it!

- **Improves Your Mood:** Spending time with positive and supportive people can make you feel happier and more optimistic. They can help you laugh away the blues and keep a smile on your face.

- **Helps You Deal with Stress:** Life throws curveballs sometimes, and having a support system can make it easier to handle the bumps in the road. They can be a listening ear when you're feeling overwhelmed and offer advice or just be there for a hug.

- **Helps You Stay Safe:** If you're being bullied, your support system can be your lifeline. They can help you develop a plan to stop the bullying, keep you safe, and make sure you know you're not alone.

A strong support system isn't just about having people to help you through tough times, it's also about celebrating the good times too! They're the ones who will be there to share your victories, big or small.

Now that you know how awesome a support system can be, let's explore who can be part of your squad! The good news is, your support system can be made up of all sorts of amazing people. Here are a few ideas:

Friends: These are the people you share secrets with, have sleepovers with, and who make you laugh until your sides hurt. True friends are there for you through thick and thin, and they can be a fantastic source of support and encouragement.

Family: Your family knows you better than anyone, and they'll always love you no matter what. Parents, siblings, grandparents, aunts, uncles, and cousins can all be part of your support system. Talk to them about what's going on in your life, and you might be surprised by the wisdom and support they can offer.

Teachers: Teachers aren't just there to teach you math and history. They can also be great mentors and confidants. If you feel comfortable talking to a teacher about something that's bothering you, like bullying, they can be a valuable source of support and guidance.

Counsellors: School counsellors are there specifically to help students with a variety of issues, including bullying. They can offer a safe and confidential space to talk about what's on your mind and develop strategies for dealing with challenges.

Mentors: Mentors are older adults who can provide guidance and support. You can find mentors through school programmes, community organisations, or even by asking a trusted adult in your life to connect you with someone they know.

Remember, your support system isn't limited to just these examples! Anyone who makes you feel good, supported, and believed in can be part of your squad.

Talking it Out: A Guide to Chatting with Your Parents

Ever feel like there's a wall between you and your parents when you need to talk? You're not alone! Talking to them about anything from school stress to personal worries can feel daunting, especially something difficult like bullying. Don't let nerves hold you back! Open communication is the magic ingredient for a strong parent-child relationship, and we're here to help you unlock those important conversations.

First things first, find the right time and place. Pick a moment when your parents seem relaxed and have some free time. Avoid interrupting them when they're busy or stressed. A private space where you won't be interrupted is ideal for an open and honest conversation.

Feeling stuck for words? Don't worry! Take some time beforehand to gather your thoughts. Brainstorm what you want to say and how you want to say it. Here are some conversation starters specifically for bullying:

- "There's something happening at school that's been making me feel uncomfortable"
- "I'm having a problem with another student, and I need your help."

By being honest about what's happening, you're taking the first step towards resolving the issue. Remember, your parents are there to support you.

Building Strong Relationships:

Strong connections with your support system are key. **Talk openly and honestly** with them about what's going on in your life. Let them know you appreciate their presence in your life. This two-way communication builds trust and strengthens your bond.

Don't Be Afraid to Ask for Help:

Sometimes it can be scary to ask for help, especially if you're worried about being labelled a 'tattletale.' But remember, asking for help is a sign of strength, not weakness. If you're being bullied, don't hesitate to reach out to a trusted adult in your support system. They can help you develop a plan to stop the bullying and keep you safe.

Building a strong support system is like constructing a fortress around yourself. It's a network of people who care about you, believe in you, and will always have your back. These connections can make you feel braver, happier, and more equipped to handle whatever life throws your way. Remember, your support system isn't just for dealing with bullies; it's there to celebrate your victories, offer a shoulder to cry on, and be your personal cheerleading squad throughout life. So **don't be afraid to reach out**, build strong relationships, and let these amazing people support you on your journey!

Now, **let's shift gears and delve into the legal side of things.** This book wouldn't be a true community legal resource guide for teens without exploring the laws and rights that protect you. In the next chapter, we'll dive into the world of teen law, empowering you with the knowledge you need to navigate situations and stand up for yourself.

Chapter Reflections

Chapter Reflections

4

Your Rights, Your Voice: Standing Up to Bullying

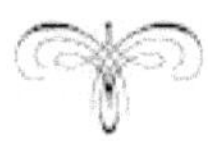

Millions of teens face bullying every year, both in person and online. But guess what? You have rights, and the law can be your ally in stopping bullying.

This chapter will equip you with the knowledge you need to understand your legal rights when it comes to bullying. We'll explore how the law can protect you **in school, online, and in your community.**

Understanding Anti-Bullying Laws

In India, there isn't one single law that specifically addresses bullying. However, there are existing legal frameworks that can be used to fight back against bullying behaviour. These include:

- **The Indian Penal Code (IPC):** This is a broad law that covers various offences. Here's how it can be relevant to bullying:

  - **Section 506 (Punishment for criminal intimidation):** This applies if someone bullies you through threats or intimidation.

  - **Example:** Imagine receiving nasty text messages that threaten you if you don't do what the bully wants. You can report this to the police under Section 506.

- **The Information Technology Act (IT Act), 2000:** This law deals with crimes committed online, including cyberbullying. Here are some relevant sections:

  - **Section 66A (Punishment for sending offensive messages by communication service):** This law says that it's a crime to deliberately share someone else's private information online without their permission. This can include things like embarrassing photos, videos, or even your home address. Imagine someone posts a mean message about you on social media and includes a picture you don't want everyone to see. Section 66E lets you take legal action against them for sharing something private without your consent.

  - **Example:** Maybe someone creates a fake social media profile to spread rumours about you. This could be a violation of Section 66A.

  - **Real World Example:** In 2020, a teenager in Delhi successfully used Section 66E against a classmate who had posted a private picture of them online. The court ordered the classmate to remove the picture and even awarded compensation to the victim for the emotional distress caused. This shows that the law can be used to hold bullies accountable for sharing private information.

It's important to remember: These are just a few examples, and the specific laws that apply will depend on the details of the bullying situation.

The Limits: It's important to remember that legal action isn't always the first answer. Sometimes, talking to a teacher or counsellor can resolve the issue. However, if the bullying is severe or involves online harassment, legal recourse can be a powerful tool.

Your Rights at School

Every student has the right to feel safe and learn in a harassment-free environment. Here's how the law can help protect you at school:

- **The Right to Education Act (RTE), 2009**: This act emphasises creating a safe and inclusive learning environment. This means your school has a responsibility to address bullying and take steps to prevent it.
- **Your Right to Report Bullying**: You have the right to report bullying to a teacher, counsellor, principal, or any other trusted adult at your school. Schools are

required to have procedures in place for reporting and investigating bullying complaints.

- **Your Right to Due Process:** If you're accused of bullying, you have the right to a fair hearing and to defend yourself.

Remember: It's important to know your school's anti-bullying policy and reporting procedures. These can usually be found in the student handbook or on the school website.

Your Rights Online (Cyberbullying)

Cyberbullying is a serious issue, and the law can help protect you online, too:

- **The IT Act (mentioned earlier):** This act can be used to address cyberbullying through offensive messages or sharing obscene content.
- **Reporting Cyberbullying:** If you're being cyberbullied, you can report it to the website or social media platform where it's happening. You can also report it to the police or a trusted adult.

Your Rights in the Community

Bullying can happen outside of school too. Here's what you should know:

- The IPC (mentioned earlier): Sections of the IPC can be applied to bullying behaviours like threats or harassment that happen in public places.

- **Real World Example:** In Mumbai, a student used Section 507 after receiving constant threatening texts from a group of classmates. The police intervened, and the bullying stopped. This shows that even offline threats can be addressed legally.

Remember: If you're being bullied in your community, don't be afraid to report it to a trusted adult or call the police.

Taking Action: What You Can Do

Knowing your rights is a powerful first step. Here are some additional tips for standing up to bullying:

- **Don't stay silent**: Report bullying to a trusted adult, school official, or the police.

- **Document everything**: Keep a record of bullying incidents, including dates, times, and details of what happened. This can be helpful if you need to take legal action.

- **Stay safe:** Avoid situations where you might be bullied and surround yourself with supportive people.

- **Empower yourself**: Learn more about your rights and resources. The more you know, the better equipped you are to handle bullying.

Being bullied can feel isolating and overwhelming. But remember, you are not alone. Millions of teens face bullying, and the law is there to protect you. By understanding your rights and knowing where to find help, you can take action against bullying and create a safer environment for yourself.

Don't be afraid to speak up! Report bullying to a trusted adult and use the resources available to you. You have the right to feel safe and respected.

This chapter has empowered you with knowledge about your legal rights when it comes to bullying. In the next chapter, we'll explore resources and support systems available to help you deal with bullying and create a positive change.

Chapter Reflections

Chapter Reflections

5

Helpline Numbers and Support Organisations

This chapter is your ultimate guide to resources and support systems designed to help you overcome bullying. Remember, you're not alone! Many organisations and websites are dedicated to creating a safe and positive learning environment for everyone.

Government Helpline:

- **Childline (1098):** This free, confidential helpline is your first point of contact for bullying-related issues. Here's a breakdown of what Childline offers:

  - **24/7 Availability:** Trained counsellors are available around the clock, every day of the year. You can reach out anytime you're feeling overwhelmed or need immediate support.

- **Confidentiality**: Your calls and interactions with Childline are completely confidential. You can talk freely about your experiences without worrying about judgement or anyone finding out.

- **Multilingual Support**: Childline counsellors can speak Hindi, English, and several other regional languages to ensure clear communication and support regardless of your location.

- **Emotional Support**: Counsellors can offer a listening ear, provide emotional support, and help you develop coping mechanisms to deal with the stress and anxiety caused by bullying.

- **Guidance and Information**: They can guide you on your rights and available resources in your area. This may include connecting you with local anti-bullying NGOs, schools offering support programmes, or even legal aid if necessary.

Here's How to Reach Childline:

- **Dial 1098**: This toll-free number can be accessed from any phone, landline, or mobile, even without balance in some cases.

- **Online Chat**: You can also chat with a counsellor online through the Childline website (https://www.

childlineindia.org/.) This can be a good option if you're uncomfortable talking on the phone.

Remember: Childline is a safe space for you to express your concerns and seek help. Don't hesitate to reach out, no matter how big or small the bullying issue might seem.

Government Cyber Security Initiatives:

While India doesn't have a single dedicated anti-bullying helpline for cyberbullying specifically, there are government initiatives aimed at improving cybersecurity and protecting users online. Here's how these initiatives can be helpful when dealing with cyberbullying:

- **Indian Computer Emergency Response Team (CERT-In)**: This government body focuses on cyber security threats and vulnerabilities. While not directly addressing cyberbullying, they offer resources and reporting mechanisms that can be helpful.

  - **Website:** https://www.cert-in.org.in

  - **Reporting Cyberbullying:** You can report cyberbullying incidents, such as online harassment or threats, through the CERT-In website. This can help them track cyberbullying trends and develop better prevention strategies.

  - **Cyber Security Awareness:** CERT-In offers resources and information on cyber security best practices. Learning how to protect your online presence and information can help prevent cyberbullying in the first place.

Important Note: Reporting cyberbullying incidents to CERT-In might not lead to immediate action against the bully. However, it contributes to a larger effort to address cyberbullying and improve online safety.

Here Are Some Additional Resources for Cyberbullying:

- **National Cyber Crime Reporting Portal:** https://cybercrime.gov.in/ This portal allows you to report various cybercrimes, including cyberbullying.
- **Cyber Crime Cells in States:** Many Indian states have established cybercrime cells within their police departments. You can search online for contact information of your local cybercrime cell if you need to report a serious cyberbullying incident that requires immediate police intervention.

Remember: Don't hesitate to seek help! These resources and support systems are here to empower you to address bullying and create a positive and safe environment for yourself and others.

Websites and Resources:

National Council of Educational Research and Training (NCERT): https://ncert.nic.in/ This government body offers a wealth of resources on preventing and addressing bullying in schools. Here's what you can find on their website:

- **Guidelines:** NCERT has developed guidelines for creating a safe and inclusive learning environment. These guidelines address bullying prevention and intervention strategies.

- **Awareness Materials:** Downloadable posters, pamphlets, and other resources can be used to raise awareness about bullying in schools.

- **Training Programmes:** NCERT offers training programmes for teachers, counsellors, and school administrators on identifying, preventing, and addressing bullying.

NGOs Supporting Bullying Prevention:

India has a vibrant network of NGOs working on anti-bullying initiatives. Here are some prominent organisations you can reach out to for help:

Guzaarish Foundation: (India, Nepal) This organisation provides support and resources to those facing bullying. They work to create a safe and compassionate world and empower individuals to stand up to bullying. Empowering students through workshops and offering a 24/7 support system via Instagram messages, Guzaarish Foundation's Bully Proof Project provides a safe space for those facing bullying. They are also launching a helpline number soon to offer even more support options.

The Aarohan Trust: https://aarohanngo.org/ works to create a safe and inclusive learning environment for children. They offer workshops, resources, and support programmes for schools and students dealing with bullying.

Pratidhi: https://ngosindia.org/delhi-ngos/pratidhi-new-delhi/ focuses on child rights and protection, including anti-bullying initiatives. They offer resources, support to victims, and even legal aid in specific cases.

The Bully Project: https://www.thebullyproject.com/ is a global organisation working to raise awareness about bullying and create positive change in schools and communities. They offer resources, workshops, and support programmes for students, parents, and teachers.

Finding Help in Your Area:

These are just a few examples, and several other NGOs work on anti-bullying initiatives across India. Here's how you can find resources in your specific area:

- **Search online:** Use keywords like 'bullying prevention NGO near me' or 'anti-bullying support + your state/city' to find organisations working in your location.
- **Talk to a trusted adult:** A teacher, counsellor, or parent can help you connect with local resources and support groups in your area.

Empowering Yourself with Knowledge:

- **Learn about your rights:** As discussed in Chapter 4, even though India doesn't have a single anti-bullying law, legal frameworks exist to address bullying behaviour. Knowing your rights empowers you to take action against bullying.

- **Download mobile apps**: Some NGOs have developed mobile apps that provide resources, helplines, and support mechanisms specifically for dealing with bullying.

Remember: Don't be afraid to reach out for help! These helplines, websites, and NGOs are here to support you and empower you to address bullying and create a positive and safe environment for yourself and others.

Conclusion: You Are Stronger Than You Think

Being bullied can be a painful and isolating experience. But remember, you are not alone. Millions of teens face bullying, but there is hope. You have the power to overcome bullying and create a safe and positive environment for yourself.

This book has equipped you with knowledge, resources, and strategies to fight back against bullying. Here's a quick recap:

- **Know Your Rights:** Chapter 4 explored how existing legal frameworks in India can be used to address bullying behaviour.

- **Help is Available:** Chapter 5 provided a comprehensive list of resources, including helplines, websites, and NGOs dedicated to supporting victims of bullying. Don't hesitate to reach out for help!

- **Empower Yourself:** Throughout this book, we've emphasised the importance of knowledge and self-awareness. Learning about your rights, building a strong support system, and taking charge of the situation are crucial steps in overcoming bullying.

Remember:

- **You are strong and capable.**

- **Your voice matters.**

- **Don't be afraid to speak up!**

By using the knowledge and resources gained from this book, you can overcome bullying and create a positive and safe future for yourself. There's a world waiting for you, a world where you can thrive and be your true self. Believe in yourself, and never stop fighting for what's right.

Chapter Reflections

Chapter Reflections

Scars That Shine: Real Stories of Rising Above Bullying

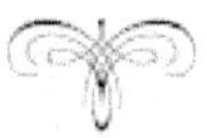

These are real stories from teenagers who faced bullying but found a way to fight back and shine. Read how they overcame the hurt and discovered their inner strength.

Story 1: The Cricket Pitch

The sting of their words, man, it was like a punch to the gut every single time. 'Loser,' they'd spit out, their laughter ringing in my ears like some twisted soundtrack to my life. Cricket used to be my escape, you know? But even that became like walking through a minefield. Every swing of the bat felt like I was trying to outrun this fear that just kept coiling tighter inside me. And then, bam, I'd end up flat on my face in that red earth, feeling like the taste of defeat was all I'd ever know. Tears would start welling up, blurring my vision of hitting that dream six I'd always wanted. It's like their jeers were hitting me harder than any physical blow, just knocking the breath right out of me when I was trying to spread my wings and fly.

But then, in the middle of all that dust and despair, there was this tiny spark of defiance. Coach saw it too. He saw this raw talent buried beneath all that fear, this fire inside me that refused to be put out. He became like my shield, always there with his unwavering belief in me, lifting me up when I felt like I was falling apart. We started these extra practice sessions, like our own little secret weapon. And slowly, that fear started to fade away, replaced by this new sense of confidence. So, the next match, every swing of that bat felt like I was making a statement. The ball? It was like it had wings, man, just flying off the bat and saying, "Yeah, take that!" to all those bullies who used to hold me down. And when I hit that winning six? Their taunts were drowned out by the cheers of the crowd. As I stood there, sweat dripping down my face, it wasn't just victory I tasted. It was this sweet satisfaction of proving them all wrong.

Story 2: Embracing My Beautiful Black Skin

The teasing didn't come from strangers; it came from the people I thought were my friends. They'd toss around the word 'Black' like it was a joke, but it felt more like a jab, wearing me down inside. I wished I could trade my skin for something lighter, envying the girls with fair complexions.

Then, my mom stepped in. She'd been through it too, facing bullies who made fun of her beautiful, dark skin. But she didn't let them win. She owned her colour, stood tall, and walked away from the negativity. Her strength became my strength. Even though I was scared of losing my so-called friends, her words gave me the courage to speak up. I faced them, demanded respect, and the laughter faded into awkward silence.

It wasn't an easy journey. I had to learn to love myself, to see the beauty in my own skin, dark and rich with history. Now, when someone tries to use 'Black' as an insult, it doesn't hurt like it used to. It's a badge of honour, a reminder of where I come from, and the strength I carry within me.

These are just snippets of the battles I've fought and won. We all have scars, reminders of the struggles we've faced. But those scars? They shine bright, showing others that they, too, can overcome the darkness. Remember, **you are not alone. Find your passion, your inner fire, and let it illuminate your path.** You are worthy, strong, and beautiful, inside and out. Don't let anyone dim your light.

You Got This: Affirmations to Fight Back Against Bullying

You are braver than you believe, stronger than you seem, and smarter than you think. And remember, you're not in this alone.

Here are some affirmations to remind yourself of your inner strength and help you rise above:

I am worthy of respect, kindness, and friendship.

My voice matters, and I will not be silenced.

I am strong, capable, and brave.

I believe in myself and my worth.

The bullies' words do not define me.

I am surrounded by people who love and support me.

I can overcome any challenge that comes my way.

I am in control of my emotions and my reactions.

I will not let bullies steal my joy.

I am beautiful, unique, and amazing just the way I am.

Repeat these affirmations to yourself every day, especially when you're feeling down or targeted. Remember, you are powerful, and you have the strength to overcome bullying.

Glossary of Bullying Terms

This glossary defines important terms related to bullying encountered throughout the book:

- **Bullying:** Repeated and deliberate harassment directed towards a person or group by someone in a position of power. This can involve physical threats or behaviours, as well as indirect and subtle forms of aggression like gossip and rumour spreading.

- **Cyberbullying:** Bullying that takes place online using electronic communication tools such as social media, text messages, or email. Common tactics include sending offensive messages, spreading rumours, or impersonating the victim.

- **Bystander:** Someone who witnesses or is aware of bullying happening to someone else. Bystanders can play a crucial role in stopping bullying by speaking up or reporting the incident.

- **Harassment:** Repeatedly sending offensive, rude, or insulting messages to someone.
- **Intimidation:** Using threats or aggressive behaviour to frighten or control someone.
- **Exclusion:** Intentionally leaving someone out of a group or activity.
- **Rumour-Spreading:** Malicious sharing of false or unconfirmed information about someone with the intent to damage their reputation or relationships.
- **Threat:** A statement expressing a serious intention to inflict harm on someone.

Legal Terms:

- **The Indian Penal Code (IPC):** A broad law that covers various offences, including sections relevant to bullying behaviours like threats or harassment.
- **The Information Technology Act (IT Act), 2000:** A law that deals with crimes committed online, including cyberbullying.

Resources:

- **Helpline:** A phone number you can call to get help or information.

- **NGO (Non-Governmental Organisation):** A non-profit organisation that works on social or environmental issues. Many NGOs work on preventing bullying and supporting victims.

"Courage is the most important of virtues because, without courage, you can't practice any other virtue consistently."

– Maya Angelou

Guzaarish Foundation Anti-Bullying and Mental Health Survey

Instructions:

Thank you for taking the time to complete this anonymous survey.Your honest responses will help us understand the experiences of teens facing bullying and mental health challenges.**We will analyse your responses and provide you with personalised resources and support.**

Please fill out this survey to the best of your ability. There are no right or wrong answers. Once you've completed the survey, you can mail it to us at **guzaarishfoundation@gmail.com**

Part 1: Bullying Experiences

1. Have you ever been bullied? (Yes / No)
2. If yes, how often are you bullied? (Daily/Weekly/Monthly/Rarely)
3. Where does the bullying typically occur? (Select all that apply)

   o At school

   o Online

   o In person outside of school

   o Other (Please specify):

4. What type of bullying do you experience most often? (Select all that apply)

   o Verbal bullying (name-calling, insults)

   o Physical bullying (hitting, shoving)

   o Socialbullying (exclusion, rumors)

   o Cyberbullying (meanmessagesonline)

   o Other (Please specify):

5. How does bullying make you feel? (Select all that apply)

   o Sad

   o Angry

   o Anxious

   o Scared

   o Helpless

   o Other (Please specify):

6. Have you ever told any one about being bullied? (Yes/No)

   - If yes,who did you tell? (Select all that apply)

   o Parent/Guardian

   o Teacher

   o Friend

   o Counselor

   o Other (Please specify):

Part 2: Mental Health

1. How would you describe your over all mood most of the time?

   o Happy

   o Sad

o Angry

o Anxious

o Other (Please specify):

2. Do you ever feel overwhelmed or stressed? (Yes/No)
3. Have you ever felt like you don't want to go to school or participate in activities you used to enjoy? (Yes/No)
4. Do you ever have trouble sleeping or eating?(Yes/No)
5. Have you ever thought about hurting yourself or others?(Yes/No)
    - If yes, please reach out for help immediately. Here are some resources:

- National Suicide Prevention Lifeline:112(India)

- Fortis Mental Health Helpline:080-46116112

- iCall (Tata Institute of Social Sciences):022-25521111

- Lifeline Foundation (Chat): https://988lifeline.org/chat/

- Sneha Foundation (Chennai): +914424640050

Part 3: Resources

- Are you aware of any resources available to help teens facing bullying?(Yes/No)
- If yes, what resources are you familiar with? (School counsellor, helpline numbers, websites)

- Would you find it helpful to have a list of state specific included in this book?(Yes/No)

Part 4: Demographics (Optional)

This section is completely optional. Answering these questions will help us understand the experiences of a wider range of teens.

1. Age:

   o 13-14 years old

   o 15-16 years old

   o 17-18 years old

   o Prefer not to answer

2. Grade Level (Optional):

   o Middle School

   o High School

   o Prefer not to answer

3. Gender Identity (Optional):

   o Male

   o Female

   o Prefer not to answer

Thank you for taking the time to complete this survey!

Personalised Resources and Support:

The Guzaarish Foundation will analyse your anonymous responses and provide you with personalised resources and support via email. This may include:

- Links to relevant helplines and support organisations in your area

- Tips and strategies for dealing with bullying and improving mental health

- Information about local support groups or therapy options

Please note: This survey and support service are completely anonymous. Your email address will not be linked to your answers.

We encourage you to reach out for help if you are being bullied or struggling with your mental health. You are not alone.

Scars That Shine: Your Personal Journal

These pages are your safe space to explore your feelings, experiences, and growth. There are no wrong answers here, just a chance to be honest with yourself and create a record of your journey.

Unmasking My Emotions

This space is judgment-free. Write down whatever comes to mind – anger, sadness, frustration, confusion. Are you being bullied? Are you witnessing bullying? What are the details of the situation?

Analyse It:

Once you've vented, take a step back. Look at your writing objectively. Who is involved? What are the specific actions happening? How does this situation make you feel physically and emotionally?

My Inner Voice

Sometimes the voice in our heads can be harsh. Write down the negative thoughts that might be swirling around.

Challenge It:

Now, challenge those thoughts! Are they realistic? Would you talk to a friend this way? Write down positive affirmations that counter the negativity. For example, if you're thinking "I'm not strong enough to deal with this," rewrite it as "I am braver than I believe."

My Support System

Who are the people you can rely on? This could be family, friends, teachers, counsellors, or even online communities. Write down their names and why they are important to you.

Reaching Out:

Sometimes, the hardest part is asking for help. Identify someone you feel comfortable talking to about what's going on. Write down what you might say to them and how their support could be helpful.

My Action Plan

It's time to take charge! Based on what you've written so far, brainstorm some strategies to address the situation. Do you need to stand up for yourself? Report the bullying? Seek emotional support? Write down specific actions you can take.

Empowering Myself:

Remember, you are not alone. Refer back to the stories and advice in "Scars That Shine" for tools and inspiration. Write down a few things you learned from the book that can empower you to move forward.

My Scars Shine Bright

This journey is about healing and growth. Imagine your scars as a symbol of your strength and resilience. Draw, write, or collage a representation of your "shining scar." This is a reminder of what you've overcome and how you are becoming the best version of yourself.

Share Your Strength (Optional):

If you feel comfortable sharing your story with others and inspiring them, you can mail your creation (drawing, writing, or collage) to us at guzaarishfoundation@gmail.com. We will post it anonymously (or with your name, if you prefer) on our Instagram page and other social media platforms to empower others facing similar challenges.

By sharing your story, you can

- Help others feel less alone.
- Show them that they are strong and can overcome bullying.
- Create a community of support and healing.

Don't worry your pretty little mind, people throw rocks at things that shine

Acknowledgements

Writing this book wouldn't have been possible without the unwavering support of some amazing people.

First and foremost, thank you Mom and Dad. Your constant support and unwavering trust meant the world to me. Mom, you didn't just support me – you motivated me. You instilled in me the importance of kindness, even towards those who weren't kind to us. You helped me become bully-proof. Dad, you're my hero. You've always pampered me (hehe!), but more importantly, you taught me the value of communication and how to be confident, even when expressing my opinions in a crowd. You're my tiger, and both of you play a crucial role in this book's existence.

Next, a huge shoutout to my brother Satvik. Even though he's in America, he never once let distance deter him from supporting me. He was always there to answer my questions, no matter how many. Thank you, Mokshi, for always being you – a true friend. And a big thank you to, Arnavi, Arushi, Aarvi, Tejas and Navika for your unwavering sibling support.

A special thank you goes to every single member of my family. Listing all your names would take a lifetime, but know that your love means the world to me. Special thanks to Mr Ravi Dhiman and Mrs Neeru Bali for offering invaluable advice that helped shape this book.

I'd also like to express my gratitude to R.J. Palacio, author of the phenomenal book "Wonder." Her work opened my eyes to the true impact of bullying and inspired me to create this resource for teens facing similar challenges.

And a big thank you to my school for those 15-minute compulsory reading periods! Back then, I never realised how much I would grow to love reading. Those 15-minutes sparked a passion for words and stories that ultimately led me to write this book.

Finally, a huge thank you to my readers. This book is for you.

Samridhi Sharma
Author

www.ingramcontent.com/pod-product-compliance
Lightning Source LLC
LaVergne TN
LVHW050338160826
845677LV00014B/3679

* 9 7 9 8 8 9 3 6 3 6 8 8 8 *